D1104300

THE GREEN MAN

A Little Book

of the

Green Man

Text and Photography by

Mike Harding

AURUM PRESS

Special edition for Past Times
First published by Aurum Press Ltd,
25 Bedford Avenue, London WC1B 3AT

Text and Photography copyright © 1998
Mike Harding

A catalogue record for this book is available
from the British Library

ISBN 1 85410 563 9

Printed in Belgium by Proost

PAST TIMES®

Facing title page – Foliate Head, Chapterhouse, York
Title page – Notre Dame, Paris
Above – Green Man, Llangym, Monmouthshire
Opposite – Green Man, Eaton under Haywood, Shropshire

I am the face in the leaves,
I am the laughter in the forest,
I am the king in the wood.
And I am the blade of grass
That thrusts through the stone-cold clay
At the death of winter.
I am before and I am after,
I am always until the end
I am the face in the forest,
I am the laughter in the leaves.

Poem by the author

INTRODUCTION

To the throbbing catechism of the buds
Cauled Lazaruth scrambles yet again,
Rehearsing the rehearsal, thrusting through
The crypt, rolls stones aside, splits husks,
And tears the swaddled cerements of the year.
– the author, from *Christ at Hardcastle Crags,* 1996

O ften labelled merely a 'grotesque' or a 'gargoyle', the Green Man can be found all over Western Europe and parts of Asia and North Africa. He is not a gargoyle, he is an archetypal image. From Mesopotamia of the third millennium BC to the close of this present era the Green Man has been there, hidden in the texts of the great epics and peering down at us from the roofs of the great cathedrals of Europe. But somewhere along the way, we seem to have lost the thread of his narrative.

I first came across the Green Man in the early 1970s when I bought the image that you can see on the facing page. It is a resin cast of a head of a Green Man and all they could tell me in the shop was that it came from a church somewhere in the south of England and that it represented a pagan fertility figure. The idea that an image which was so overtly pagan in origin could appear in Christian churches intrigued me and started me off on a quest which has not yet ended, the quest for the meaning of the Green Man.

During the last twenty-five years I have searched for him all over the British Isles and in places much further afield. I have found mention of him in the medieval English poem *Gawain and the Green Knight* and in the Epic of Gilgamesh, where Enkidu and Gilgamesh behead the Guardian of the Forest with terrible results. As the god that dies and is born again he appears in mythology as Dionysos, Osiris, Odin, Tamuz and Jesus Christ. As John Barleycorn he is the Corn Spirit who dies and is reborn each year. He stares down from the door of Chartres Cathedral and smiles from the pillar of a Jain temple in Rajasthan. He can be seen dancing ahead of the May Queen in procession on May Day at Knutsford in England and in Borneo he is found painted on the walls of Christian churches. He is probably as old as mankind itself, always there, hidden in the woods, peering from the leaves. Puck, Jack in the Green, the Old Man of the Woods or simply the Green Man: we know him without understanding him.

There are four main types of Green Man: the foliate head in which the face becomes leaves, the spewing or uttering head where leaves and foliage emerge from the mouth (as in the example above from Beverley Minster), the 'bloodsucker' head where branches and leaves spring from the eyes and ears as well as the mouth, and Jack in the Green which is often simply a head peering at us out of a frame of foliage. There are no definite lines of demarcation however and you will often find images that display characteristics of more than one type; it is common for example to find spewing heads in which the flesh is also turning into foliage as in the golden head, here, on a roof boss from Canterbury Cathedral.

One common theme unites them all however and that is the communion or fusion between man and the vegetable world. All flesh is grass, and the Green Man, perhaps better than any other image illustrates the principle of death and corruption, resurrection and re-birth.

The name of the Green Man has long been a subject of some debate. Lady Raglan first used the term to describe the head at Llangwm, likening it to the *Green Man or Jack in the Green* of the inn signs and the May Day processions. But the term is much older although the masons and woodcarvers who cut the faces may have called him a different name altogether. What we do know for certain is that figures called Green Men went about in procession during the Middle Ages and were covered in foliage and greenery. In the absence of any better evidence the term Lady Raglan used will have to suffice.

Industry and science have done more to transform the western world in the last one hundred years than all the changes of the previous two thousand. We look all about us at a polluted and scarred earth, BSE, overcrowded cities, the greenhouse effect – we are presented with a seemingly hopeless case. Yet to many, the Green Man, this union of the human and the green world shows us a possible way out. As many have said, perhaps our awakening awareness of him is a last chance to put right the damage we have caused.

The Green Man has a story to tell us – if only we knew how to listen.

THE ARCHETYPAL GREEN MAN

❖

Fountains Abbey, North Yorkshire

Kathleen Basford was a botanist working at Manchester University when she came across the head on the opposite page carved into a keystone on one of the windows of the chapel of the Nine Altars at Fountains Abbey in 1964. Fascinated by what she calls 'an image of death and ruin' she began a search that took her the best part of her lifetime and took her all over England and the continent, as far eastwards as Istanbul.

In 1978 she published *The Green Man* (D.S. Brewer, reissued in paperback 1998), which is still the definitive work on the image. Thoughtful, impeccably researched and without any of the wilder references to crop circles, ley lines or 'Celtic' subjects such as Cernunos whom many have tried to link to the Green Man, it is the standard reference for anybody seriously interested in the subject.

On the obverse of the keystone looking down into the chapel at Fountains Abbey is the angel you see on this page. The Green Man is outside the building facing the rising sun, the angel within, scroll in his hand. Does the Angel represent the revealed truth of the Scriptures, and the Green Man the unredeemed soul of mankind looking to the light?

Angels & Green Men

Rosslyn Chapel, Rosslyn, Edinburgh

Rosslyn Chapel was built by William Sinclair in the fifteenth century and is one of the strangest churches I have ever visited, incredibly ornate, almost to the point of decadence and home to legends of murdered apprentice masons, buried treasure and the Holy Grail.

Sinclair was an important member of the Knights Templar, a militant monastic order founded around 1123 to protect the routes of pilgrimage to the Holy Land. Exempt from most laws and answerable only to the Pope himself, they rapidly spread across Europe and the Holy Land and became so wealthy that the King of France actually borrowed money from them to prop up his throne. Small wonder that they were dissolved and their leaders tortured and burnt at the stake in 1307, accused amongst other things of sodomy and of worshipping an idol called Baphomet.

After their dissolution many Templars are supposed to have fled to Scotland. This would explain the connection with William Sinclair and the fact that there are said to be 103 images of the Green Man in Rosslyn Chapel and only one of Jesus.

ROOF BOSSES

❖

York Arts Centre

York Arts Centre was formerly St Mary's Church, one of the many medieval churches of that most medieval of all cities.

The roof bosses of the building have recently been repainted and amongst them is the tongue-pulling Lion spewing leaves on the facing page. 'Green' cat heads and lion heads are not uncommon and there is even a Green Dog in the church of St Mary Redcliffe, Bristol, but this head in York is particularly interesting in that close by is a boss with what seems to be a coat of arms, perhaps belonging to a guild or craft such as the Mercers.

I sent a photograph of the shield to Andrew Sinclair, author of *The Templars and the Grail*, who assured me that the symbols were of Templar origin.

I have long wondered about a connection between the Knights Templar and the Green Man but, although I have evidence that the head was being carved in their Jerusalem workshops in the twelfth century and the richness of the Green Man carvings in Rosslyn Chapel (pp.16–17) would point to some connection, I am still wary of making any pronouncements. It remains an interesting puzzle.

GREEN MAN & MAGIC THORN

❖

Sutton Benger, Wiltshire

Perhaps one of the great works of art of Western Europe, the position of this beautifully carved head in such a small church still remains a mystery. Dated by Pevsner to the Middle Ages, the naturalism of the face and the intricacy of the carving have prompted some scholars to doubt its antiquity. Yet there are many equally intricate carvings in contemporary cathedrals across Europe.

Was it brought here from a larger church destroyed at the Reformation? Was it created at the behest of a wealthy benefactor?

We have no way of knowing, any more than we know what image (the Virgin Mary?) this plinth supported.

The Sutton Benger Green Man has hawthorn issuing from his mouth and birds eating the berries. The hawthorn is one of the most magical of all trees, witches' broomsticks were garlanded with 'may', the flower of the thorn, and the beginning of Beltane, the festival of the death of winter, was determined not by the calendar date but by its blossoming. To this day, in parts of rural Ireland farmers will divert a road they are making rather than cut down a 'whitethorn' bush.

Green Men in Anguish

❖

Exeter, Devon & Beverley, Yorkshire

As though in pain or torment both the spewing head on this page, from Exeter Cathedral, and the foliate head opposite from Beverley Minster represent a subspecies of the Green Man, the head in anguish. Kathleen Basford was deeply moved by this aspect of the Green Man and felt that it was one of the dominant features of the image.

The despair expressed in some of the faces is even more disquieting because the images appear so human.

It is difficult for us to know what the expression on the faces of the Green Men *in extremis* are meant to convey. Perhaps it is an expression of the fact that, as a medieval poem says, 'all greenness comes to withering' and what we are looking at are the faces of the dead from whose mouths and flesh new life springs? Or are the heads meant to represent demons trapped for eternity by the vegetable and therefore material world, the world of the flesh and the devil? Interestingly, though it has been suggested by some historians that all Green Men are devils or demons, very few of them are shown with horns.

FRUITFUL GREEN MEN

❖

Beverley, Yorkshire & Exeter, Devon

Roman columns of the sixth century AD show the Green Man as a foliate head, and until the appearance of spewing heads on later tombs and the carvings in twelfth-century Romanesque churches, that seems to have been the dominant form.

By the thirteenth century the carved heads of Chartres Cathedral were spouting recognisable acanthus and vine leaves and bunches of grapes can be found hanging from the mouths of several of the Chartres heads.

As a symbol of fecundity the Green Man seems to have readily and rapidly found his way into the vocabulary of the stone-masons and woodcarvers of the Middle Ages.

The crude but jolly head opposite from Bristol with its shining bunch of luscious grapes is very different to some of the more demonic and threatening heads, while the cheerful little chap on this page with his crazed grin is sprouting oak leaves and acorns in fine fashion from scalp and ears.

Victorian Heads

Nantwich, Cheshire

When Gilbert Scott restored the porch of St Mary's Nantwich he had sense enough to recognise the force of custom and tradition and have some new Green Man heads cut by the stone masons.

The soft red sandstone, the same kind of stone that was used in the building of Chester and Carlisle Cathedrals, takes a cut well and in the case of the two heads here, their being inside means that they will not be subject to the acid rain and pollution that has scarred so many of the churches in the area.

The spewing head on the page facing is an archetypal demonic head with luscious leaves flowing from his mouth. The head on this page is almost maniacal with his rabid grin and flowing mane of hair.

Nantwich contains a number of Green Men including these here, in the porch, a poupee and a fragment of glass from an old Benedictine monastery. The town lies close by what was once the ancient forest of Delamere and leads me to wonder yet again whether there is any connection between the Green Man as a symbol perhaps of the old Guardian of the Forest, and of the woods that were cleared to build the medieval churches and cathedrals.

Romanesque Heads

❖

Leominster, Shropshire & Kilpeck, Herefordshire

Biting, snapping and chewing heads are to be found in the pages of many medieval illustrated manuscripts. The Book of Kells and the Lindisfarne Gospels contain scores of examples. In many cases the faces are linked with spirals and whorls of foliage,

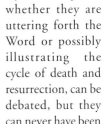

the branches and flowers forming part of the letters or acting as a frame around a letter. It is almost as though the mouth has assumed a significance beyond that of merely eating, drinking and speaking.

Nothing that appears in medieval art is without its own narrative. The meaning of the images you see on these pages, which seem to me to have been directly influenced by manuscript art, whether they are uttering forth the Word or possibly illustrating the cycle of death and resurrection, can be debated, but they can never have been 'mere grotesques' as some have called them. The lovely Romanesque church at Kilpeck has the Green Man above as a capital on its famous door, the carving from Leominster, opposite, with the foliage returning again into the head is a type often found in the letters and margins of manuscripts.

Roof Boss & Leaf Head

❖

Abbey Dore, Herefordshire

Abbey Dore lies in one of the most beautiful valleys in Herefordshire. Once a great Cistercian monastery built during the early years of the thirteenth century, the building was almost completely destroyed during the dissolution of the monasteries and the years of neglect that followed. By the time that Lord Scudamore began his restoration in 1633 the whole of the nave had fallen into ruin. Of the 250-foot long church only the crossing, transepts and chancel remain.

At the east end of the chancel in amongst heap of carvings and mouldings is the magnificent head you see on the opposite page, a deposed roof boss from what was once the great nave.

The Cistercian Order, under its founder St Bernard, was, in its earliest years, against ornamentation of any kind in its churches. In later years decoration began to appear and it is interesting how much the Green Man features in subsequent Cistercian abbeys.

The head on this page is one of a pair on a Jacobean screen and was in all probability carved at the direction of Lord Scudamore. This must surely indicate that, even at this late date, the Green Man still carried a great deal of significance and meaning.

GREEN MAN & WHEEL OF LIFE

Much Marcle, Herefordshire

St Bartholomew's, Much Marcle, is a fascinating church with a number of Green Men and other carvings all cut into the same finely grained golden stone.

The head on the facing page is perhaps the most intriguing of them all in that, not only is he

beautifully carved, but he is the only Green Man, so far as I know, wearing jewellery or ornamentation of any kind, in this case having a sunwheel hanging on a chain from his neck.

The sunwheel, a cross within a circle, is one of the oldest symbols known to man. The cross represents the enmeshing of time and space, and the crossing of night and day, while the circle represents both the sun and the eternal nature of the spirit world. It is a symbol often found in alchemy and is a mystic symbol in many other world cultures.

The carving on this page, a capital on another pillar, has no jewels or finery but is another beautifully carved example of the most common Green Man type, the head spewing out or uttering greenery.

Jack & the May King

Southwell Minster, Nottinghamshire

Perhaps the clearest representation of a Jack-in-the-Green figure that we have, the head opposite, carrying his bower of leaves, like the Jack who could be seen in the May Day Revels until Victorian times, is one gem amongst many others in the chapterhouse of Southwell Minster.

One of the world's great works

of art, the chapterhouse is more like an arboretum cut from stone than a room. Foliage so finely carved that you suspect the wind could make it tremble and sway entwines round every column and arch, and many of the major plants and trees of Britain are cut out of the stone; hawthorn: hemp, nettle, ivy, bryony, hop, maple, vine, oak, buttercup, rose and mulberry.

The Green Man on this page, with his fleur de lys crown and the hawthorn leaves shooting from his forehead and chin has earned the title of the May King, because the hawthorn bears the may blossom, the symbol of the coming of summer.

Green Cat Heads

Tiverton, Devon & Knighton, Powys, Wales

Cats spewing foliage appear in the margins of medieval manuscripts, often as the ascenders and descenders of illuminated letters. The cat was associated in the medieval mind with darkness and the night and thus with things sinister. It therefore became  a symbol of both evil and base cunning, hence the association of cats with witches, tall hats and broomsticks.

Whether Green Cats are supposed to be evil things of darkness is questionable; the head above appears on the overmantle of a seventeenth-century farmhouse near Knighton and I was told that it had always been seen as bringing good luck on the house.

The Tiverton cat on the facing page is a wild-looking moggy with more than a dash of the human in his nose and eyes. He glares down from his capital into the body of the church, spewing foliage but, though he looks fairly frightening and impish I find it hard to see him as wicked or evil.

Although there are a great number of Green Cats all over Europe, there is, as far as I know, only one Green Dog, high up in the ceiling of St John's Chapel in the lovely St Mary Redcliffe.

Snake Head & Lion Head

Hereford Cathedral & Appleby, Cumbria

Serpents and dragons are found as companions to the Green Man at a number of sites but it is rare that we see Green Serpents as such in their own right.

The little Green Snake from Appleby with the human head and cat ears, opposite, is now part of a pew that was made in more recent years from a Jacobean oak organ case. The snake is spewing out foliage, a branch of which becomes its tail so that, like Ouroboros the serpent that swallows its own tail, it is a symbol of totality, rebirth, immortality and the round of existence. The image appears in ancient Greece and Egypt and is also found in alchemy. How fitting that Ouroboros and the Green Man should be so linked.

The jolly lion, embodying the wisdom and energy of the animal kingdom is from Hereford Cathedral. This kind of image is more common and again illustrates the link between the animal and vegetable worlds.

GUARDIAN OF THE FOREST

❖

Apo Kayan, Borneo

Perhaps a Lord God of the Forest, this elaborate foliate head is seen everywhere in the Apo Kayan area of Borneo as a protecting deity. It appears above doors and on walls and even woven into the fabric of the baskets used by the women for carrying their babies.

He is no longer found on the coast of Malaysia since that area is mainly Muslim, but inland he appears in many places, even on the walls of recently built Catholic churches – an indication of how the image also came to be accepted in medieval Christian Europe?

It is possible that this image is a local version of Kirtimukha, the head found in Jain temples in India. An eastward migration of the symbol is quite feasible since both Buddhism and Islam found their way into this area following the trade routes. As is often pointed out interpretations are culture specific but the images themselves are not. The sunwheel found in Buddhist temples became the swastika of the Nazis; one symbol, two totally opposite meanings.

The photographs on these two pages were taken by a Dutch friend.

GREEN MISERICORDS

❖

Southwell Minster & Ludlow, Shropshire

Misericords are the little ledges under the tip-up seats in the choir stalls in many European cathedrals and churches. When the seat is tipped up the ledge provides a small resting place for the monks who would otherwise have to stand through the long hours of the services. Misericord is Latin and comes from the two words for pity and heart, implying, I suppose, that the poor monks were being accorded a little pity.

A popular subject with misericord carvers, the Green Man appears in a great many collections. The fine chap opposite is one of two roundel supporters from a stall in the fine fifteenth-century church of St Laurence, Ludlow. They are carved either side of a chained hart, which itself is thought to be a representation of Christ. The seated Green Man on this page from the lovely minster at Southwell is one of the few full-bodied Green Men for, in all but a handful of cases, the image appears as a head only (see also p. 65).

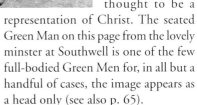

GOLD & GREEN

❖

Paris, France & Bolton Abbey, Yorkshire

In the heart of the Ile de la Cité in Paris is the Church of Ste Chapelle. There, the head on the opposite page, one of the most striking Green Men in France, supports the statue of St James, the brother of Christ.

Beyond the statues of the apostles and the ornate gilded foliage there is little other decoration in the chapel. Only the Green Man smiles enigmatically out across the church, from within his mask of leaves.

The Green Man on this page stares down balefully from high in the roof

of the priory church at Bolton Abbey on the banks of the River Wharfe.

In medieval churches the statues would all have been painted in bright colours, the walls would have been covered with paintings and some of the most important images such as those of Christ or the Virgin would have been gilded.

The fact that these Green Men, like those at Tewkesbury Abbey were gilded would suggest that, like the gilded images in Byzantine art, they have a venerable or even heavenly aspect.

Bench End Green Men

❖

Bishops Lydeard, Somerset

Somerset has a great number of Green Men, many of them, like the one on this page, carved into the ends of pews.

These very simple faces and foliage dating from the fifteenth century are

nevertheless extremely important, carved, as they were, in such prominent and accessible places.

Unlike many Green Men that are hidden on high in roof bosses or on capitals, the bench ends are close to ground level and would have been immediately on view to everybody entering the church.

Only in Somerset is this tradition of carved pew-ends so wide-spread and it would appear that the same carvers worked on a number of churches in the area. The carving opposite, with its background of red is from another bench end in the same church.

While I was photographing these images a lady who was in the church arranging flowers came up to me quietly and, making sure that nobody else heard, whispered: 'It's nice to see that he's being accepted again, isn't it?'

GREEN MAN ROUNDELS

❖

Halse, Somerset
& Eaton under Haywood, Shropshire

It is quite unusual to find such a three-dimensional subject as the Green Man treated in an almost two-dimensional way but in the two roundels here it has been done with great delicacy and not a little humour.

The carving opposite from the thirteenth century church of St James at Halse is a lovely depiction of a head breathing out foliage, with more sprouting from the middle of his brow.

The head on this page is one of my favourite foliate heads and reminds me ever so much of Fat Freddy's Cat in the under-ground American comic of the same name. The smiling face is so full of mischief that I wonder whether what we are looking at here is the Green Man in his role as Puck or Robin Goodfellow, both of whom could well be descendants of the great god and guardian of the woods, Pan.

Tibetan Buddhist Heads

Kathmandu, Nepal & Dankhar, Spiti, North India

High up in the Indian Himalayas, close to the Tibetan border the chapels of Dhankar Gompa have a great number of wall paintings including the fine image on this page of a Green Man-type figure that may have come  originally from Chinese fire-dragon images of the Bronze Age.

The horned semi-human, semi-dragon figure that appears on so many bronzes of that period may well be the precursor of the Christian Satan who is often shown with horns and the body of a serpent or a dragon. I asked a Buddhist monk what was coming from the mouth and he replied 'Trees'.

The horns on the heads can be interpreted as the attributes of a demon yet both Moses and Alexander the Great are sometimes shown wearing horns, in this case to indicate the attainment of wisdom, horns also being the sign of the shaman. The beautiful flowers and stylized leaves in the painting from Kathmandu, opposite, indicate that what is coming from the mouth of the horned Green Man is the whole of the vegetable world.

GOLDEN HEADS ON HIGH

❖

Tewkesbury Abbey, Gloucestershire

The abbey at Tewkesbury has a great number of Green Men, some of them re-gilded recently like the face opposite which, seemingly in agony, stares down into the body of the church.

The head on this page with the leaves swirling from its mouth is one of several in Tewkesbury Abbey featuring finely carved leaves; in this carving the leaves and acorns of the oak are clearly visible.

The oak, with its great strength and longevity, was a tree sacred to the Celtic and Norse peoples and seems to have been the subject of special veneration up to this century.

In Devon, until fairly recent times, there were what locals called 'dancing trees', giant oaks that the people would encircle and dance around on days of high festival.

In the Middle Ages, Tewkesbury, like Devon, would have been a richly forested part of the country and perhaps again the care and attention lavished on the carvings indicate the Green Man's manifestation as a wood spirit or Guardian of the Forests.

WOODEN BOSSES

❖

Spreyton & Bampton, Devon

Tongue-pullers, like the Green Man opposite with leaves flowing from his ears, may be pure fertility symbols – since the tongue we see in medieval iconography is said by some scholars to represent the penis. If this is so then it ties in well with the idea of the Green Man as a representation of fecundity since another meaning of 'green' is 'lusty' or 'fecund'.

The fleur de lys on the forehead could denote kingship or be a reference to the pagan magical symbol of the three, perhaps also indicating the Christian doctrine of the Trinity.

Devon has a tremendous number of Green Men, many appearing in churches in villages ending in 'nympton', a form of 'nemeton', the word denoting an ancient sacred grove. Typically, many of the heads are carved on wooden bosses in the oldest of the county's churches.

The Green Man head on this page from Spreyton has been taken over completely by the vegetable world. This is a typical example of the mysterious and quite fearsome 'Bloodsucker' type of carving.

ITALIANATE LEAF MASKS

❖

Paris, France & Tunstall, Lancashire

By the time he arrived in Italy the Green Man in his foliate form had become quite stylized. On the opposite page he looks out from the rim of a twelfth-century Italian plate on which the hanged body of a woman – like the hanged man of the Tarot pack – is a centre-piece. The rim of

the plate, which can be seen in the Louvre Museum, Paris, contains several Green Men as well as items of militaria.

The heads on this page are from a stained glass window in the tiny parish church of Tunstall near Kirkby Lonsdale and are a lovely example of the influence of Italian art in the Middle Ages. The window is of Flemish origin, and the two foliate masks here echo the classical leaf masks found on second-century Roman columns.

During the Dionysian revels merrymakers stuck vine leaves on their faces in honour of Bacchus, the god of wine. Such images, first carved on temple columns, travelled from the Mediterranean across Europe to appear in a stained-glass window in a remote but pretty corner of Lancashire.

Anglo-Indian Foliate Heads

❖

Delhi Museum, India & Beverley Minster, Yorkshire

Dating from eighth-century Rajasthan, the Green Man on the opposite page is from a Jain Temple. It is a pure foliate head, the flesh turning into curled leaves, the eyes looking sagely out. How the Green Man came to appear in so many diverse places at so many different times is still a mystery. Heads from the Lebanon and Iraq can be dated to the second century AD and there are early Romanesque heads in eleventh-century Templar churches in Jerusalem. From the twelfth to the fifteenth centuries heads appeared in cathedrals and churches across Europe.

Could it be that stonecarvers migrated westwards from Asia Minor taking their skills and some of their images with them? The head on this page is on a capital in Beverley Minster; it is surely no coincidence that the two images here are so similar.

The movement of skilled craftsmen across Europe and Africa may have been far more widespread than we imagine and cultural artefacts, as part of trade and warfare, moved great distances. However it came about, the Green Man was certainly not confined to a small corner of Europe.

Stained-Glass Green Men

❖

Notre Dame, Paris & St Mary Redcliffe, Bristol

Close by the treasury in the north wall of the choir of Notre Dame is a window restored by Viollet le Duc in the mid-nineteenth century.

The head opposite is one of many lustrous Green Men in the window and was described to the author as *'le diable de la foret'* by a cathedral attendant, a possible Christian demonization of a pagan theme. Further along the island on which Notre Dame stands is the Square du Vert Galant, the place of the 'green' or lusty, gallant or knight, named in honour of Henri IV, whose statue rides at the island's prow. He was renowned for being *'toujours un vert galant'* and the connection between kingship and fertility is an old one, the health and fecundity of the king being the prime factor in the safety and stability of the nation.

The crowned head above is one of the few stained-glass Green Men in the British Isles. Like many other pieces in the window of St John's Chapel in St Mary's, it is badly damaged. Looking at such windows, we can only guess at the lovely treasures that Henry VIII and Oliver Cromwell managed to destroy during their miserable reigns.

JAIN GREEN MAN & TREE

❖

Qutb Minar, New Delhi, India
& Ranakpur, Rajasthan

The Jain Temple at Ranakpur is a breathtaking marble forest with a lacework of stone spanning arch after arch and ornate carvings hanging from the ceiling like clusters of fruit. On one of the columns is the Green Man opposite, with birds in the stylized branches of his 'tree' like those in the branches at Sutton Benger.

Jains have an incredible respect for all living things, and their temples are filled with images of animals, birds, flowers and swirling foliage.

The carving opposite, more than any other I saw in India, convinced me that there was either a movement of images which changed their inter-pretation as they became part of the culture of the host country or that there is simply a common unconscious core in all humanity that recognizes and creates the Green Man over and again in various guises.

The head on this page from Delhi could be either chained to the material world or uttering the word or 'logos' of creation. Interestingly, the Jain Temple of Qutb Minar was converted to a mosque during the Mogul reign and though all other decoration was smashed off the Green Men were left completely untouched.

GUARDIAN GREEN MEN

❖

Kathmandu, Nepal & Linley, Shropshire

Apotropaic carvings like the Green Men here serve to ward off evil and to guard the buildings they stand over from any incursion of demons or negative powers.

The head opposite with the marigolds pouring from its mouth stands watch above a statue of the Buddha in the temple of Swayambunath Gompa in Nepal. The carving on this page can be found spewing out a small forest on a tympanum above the north door of the little church of St Leonards in Linley.

One of the few full-bodied Green Men, he stands facing out over what is often known as the Devil Door, so-called for two reasons: it was left open at baptism so that any devils in the child would be driven out that way, and also it was believed that the north side of the church was the sinister side facing the dark and it was from that direction that all forms of evil came.

Christ & A Leaf Man

Sampford Courtenay, Devon &
Eaton under Haywood, Shropshire

A wild staring leaf man whose face looks out from its frame of leaves, the carving opposite is one of a fine set of foliate heads in the small but atmospheric church at Eaton under Heywood. Kathleen Basford, whose work has inspired so many searchers in their quest for the Green Man, concluded that 'the imagery can be ambivalent. The Green Man can be at once both beautiful and sinister.' The carving above, looking for all the world like the head of the dead Christ is perhaps the loveliest of all the Devon wooden roof bosses.

What are we to make of carvings like these? Are they doomed and lost souls? Are they demons? Are they perhaps the spirits of the forest looking out at us from their green flowering? Or are they the souls of the dead looking at us out of the decay of the vegetable world? Perhaps they are really all of these things and more.

My thanks go to the Deans and Chapters of all the cathedrals whose treasures are featured in this book and likewise to all the vicars, vergers and enthusiastic helpers who gave me so much assistance. Draughty churches and chapels were opened for me and people went to great lengths to light my way in the darkness. Countless ladies gave me cups of coffee and tea and, with the exception of one man who is obviously unwell, I was shown nothing but kindness and courtesy by all those involved in the care and maintenance of the churches and cathedrals they so obviously love. I offer this book as my thanks to them and in praise of the men and women who created such great art to the glory of their God. Special thanks are due to Ank and Jeff, two Dutch friends who kindly loaned me the shots from Apo Kayan and to Kathleen Basford whose wonderful letters and enthusiastic wisdom have been a constant encouragement.

The photographs were taken using a Nikon F3 and 20mm, 35mm, 600mm and 55mm macro lenses. The film used throughout was Fuji Velvia and I also used a small video light to illuminate some of the carvings

This lovely leafy-headed Green Man
is a detail from a large stained-glass window
in Notre Dame de Paris; opposite is a roof boss
from Tewkesbury Abbey, (see pp. 52–53).

THE END